The Poetry of John Payne

Volume IV - Salvestra

John Payne was born on 23rd August 1842 in Bloomsbury, London.

He began his career in the legal profession but thus was soon put to one side as he began his renowned translations of Boccaccio's Decameron, The Arabian Nights, and then the poets Omar Khayyam, François Villon and Diwan Hafez. Of the latter, who he ranked in the same bracket as Dante and Shakepeare, he said; he takes the "whole sweep of human experience and irradiates all things with his sun-gold and his wisdom"

Later Payne became involved with limited edition publishing, and the Villon Society, which was dedicated to the poems of François Villon who was Frances' best known poet of the middle Ages and unfortunately also a thief and a murderer.

John Payne died on 11th February, 1916 at the age of 73 in South Kensington, London.

Index of Contents

SALVESTRA

Ah love, thou art but as a Summer's guest,
That long before the Winter fleest away
And in some warmer haven harbourest,
Nipt by the hard swift life of our Today!
Our love is scant and flowerless as our May
And will not lightly let its pinions soil
Their rainbow plumes in our unblissful toil.

Time was, fair God, when thou heldst fuller sway
And all folk were thy thralls in gentilesse:
Time was when men were simpler than today
And life was not one fierce and loveless stress
Of unrelenting labour in the press
Of joyless souls, when men had leave to rest
And toy with grace and beauty, unreprest.

Full sweet, ah! hopeless sweet, to us it seems—
Fast bounden in a mesh of strife and care—
That time of graceful ease and builded dreams,
Seen in a glamour through the misted air;

Through which sweet strains of song the breezes bear
And scents of flowers that then were full and blythe
But now are mown away by Timers swift scythe.

And yet it was no golden age, that time;
Not unalloyed with pain and doubt and strife:
But through all ventures ran the gold of rhyme
And Love was high and was the Lord of Life.
From Venice-turrets unto Algarsife,
All held fair deeds and lovely worshipful
And all were scholars in Lovers gracious school.

Then men did honour Love with heart and soul,
Setting their lives upon his smile or frown;
For in their hearts his altar-flame was whole
And burnt unchanged until Life's sun went down.
Love was the flower of life and honour's crown,
Wherewith men perfumed all the weary years
And purged the air from mean and sordid fears.

Then men, as they for very Love could live,
So for the death of very Love could die,
Holding it shame to let the rank flesh give
Commandment to the swift soul's fantasy;
And for the love of him they held so high,
Did woo and win, with fair and potent faith,
The cold embraces of his brother Death.

A sad sweet tale is hovering in my thought,
A tale of perfect love in death fulfilled,
From out the waves of sweeping Time upwrought
By that enchanter of the pasty who filled
The ears of men with music sweet and wild,
When in the world he breathed strange scents upon
That sheaf of flowers men call Decameron.

A tale in dreams, heard betwixt wake and sleeps
Under the tremulous shadow of the planes;
Attuned to rhythmic cadence by the sweep
Of murmurous rillets through the scented lanes
Of rose and jasmine, sweep of wings and strains
Of happy linnets piping to the rose
And chirp of crickets in the olive-close.

O Master, of whose speech in that green time,
Heard under shredded laurels and faint flowers,
I took the echo for my painful rhyme,
To warm it in this cold hard time of ours,

Whose plagues no wall of rose or lys outbowers—
Let not thy laureat brow be rough with frown,
If I unleavè thy honeysuckle crown

With my interpreting. Sweet is the will,
And all fair-meaning as a day in June,
The faded decor ds of thy song to fill
And echo back that magical sweet tune
Thou sangest in the garden's golden noon,
With youths and maidens lying, myrtle-crowned,
Upon the flower-glad carpet of the ground.

But ah! the air is faint with weariness
Of toil and love is grown a doubtful dream,
That now no longer, type of holiness,
Regilds the shapes of faded things that seem
And are not in our world! The sad ghosts stream
Toward the darkness; and my sense can seize
No touch of reverent peace or grateful ease,

No waft of tender fancy in the sky,
No Phoebus standing, dawn-red, on the hill—
And must e'en feed itself on memory
And with those strains of old its yearning fill.
Whose echo at my heart-strings lingers still—
Unable to revive the ancient flame.
Sadly some phantom of its brightness frame.

Fair flowery city, peerless in the world,
Germ-garden of the golden blooms of Art,
But seldom have thy myrtle-groves impearled
So fair a creature in their flowerful heart
As young Salvestra. Could my song impart
Her manifold perfections, well I deem
My verse should glow with glories of a dream.

So fair she was, there is no rose so fair
That in the noon drinks colour from the sun:
No flower could match the hyacinths of her hair,
Fresh from the webs of night and morning spun:
Her eyes were lakes, whereon, when day is done.
The slow night comes with halt and timorous pace.
And dim dreams fill the enchanted interspace.

There was the house of dreams; and on her brow—

Clear as the marge of that cool well where Pan
Was wont to play with Pitys—broad and low
With trellised ringlets — ended and began
All glamours that can charm the heart of man:
There was the crystal dwelling of the Loves
And there bright Venus fed her golden doves.

What hues can paint her mouth, what words express
The ivory shaft of her most perfect throat?
And what her bosom's rounded perfectness?
That with the heaving breath did swell and float,
As if its snows had lately learnt by rote
The rapturous carol of some woodland bird
And to the cadence ever mutely stirred.

The very sun did gently look on her
And only kissed, not burnt, her crystal brows:
Among her locks the flower-breathed winds did stir
And filled them with the perfumes of the rose
And scents of foreign sweets that no man knows.
But haply ravished from those plains of spice
That lengthen out the glades of Paradise.

So fair she was, her sight had virtue in 't:
The vision of her face was used to stir
Strange deeps of love. Full many a heart of flint
Was softened, when men's eyes did look on her:
Like violets in the morning of the year,
There was a perfume went from her that drew
Men's careworn souls to tender thoughts and true.

If all things loved her, even the fierce son,
And breezes for her wooing came from for,
How should Girolamo's young bosom shun
The keen sweet shaft of Love's unpardoning star,
Wherewith so many hearts enwounded are?
Or how play traitor to the general fate,
He, whom the heavens had surely made for mate

Of that unparagoned brightness? If on earth
The gods had guerdoned and appointed one
To be conjoined with her in house of birth,
Girolamo was sure that Fortune's son.
His life, with hers in equal hour begun,
Had from the same breast drawn its aliment
And all the currents of their youth were blent

Within a common channel. Childhood was

Dual for them with doubled love and pain;
And with unseparate course the years did pass
For them along the primrose-tufted plain
Of early youth; till, when the rise and wane
Of the recurrent Springs began to tend
Toward that spot where times of childhood end.

Where laughing girl puts on grave womanhood
And youth is sudden man, the innocent ties,
That had so long entwined the two, renewed
Their power. As thought grew in Salvestra's eyes.
The ancient childish amity did rise
In his young breast the olden banks above
And swelled into a deep and passionate love.

If she was dark as Night and vague and rare
As star-bright evening, thick with netted lights,
He was as frank and bright and golden-fair
As a May mom, when on the sapphire heights
Of heaven the young day comes with all delights
And tender glories of the dewy dawn
And wild flowers wake on every woodland lawn.

It seemed the sun shone always (m his brow,
Among his locks' full-clustered tender gold.
Whose every shadow with rich light did glow;
And his true eyes were cast in passion's mould,
So fair a deep of love, all aureoled
With hope, did lurk within their amethyst,
Whose lids Diana might have stooped and kiss'd.

There looked from out his face so dear a Spring
Of love and youth, so pure and undefiled
By care or baseness, that no birds that sing
Among the trellis—when the boughs are piled
With blossom and the sweet lush vines run wild
With early dusters—cared to hide from him.
If to the carol of their morning hymn

He crept to listen through the flush of flowers;
No fawn but laid the velvet of its mouth
Upon his beckoning hand: the fear that sours
All creatures at man's aspect ('spite the drouth
Of love that habits all the sunny South)
Fled from him, as the plague flies from the breath
Of some sweet fragrance, enemy to Death.

There was in him a candid fearlessness

And frank delight of love, that drew men back,
Regarding him, from out the cheerlessness
Of modem life, along the dim years' track.
To the dd age, when hate nor fear nor rack
Of rueful discord held the enchanted air,
But all were loving, kind and debonair;

When love was not a virtue, but a sense,
A natural impulse of untainted souls.
That had no thought of praise or recompense
For what was but an instinct, and the goals,
Tow'rd which our life's sore-troubled current rolls,
Had not yet darkened all the innocent air
With lurid lights of greed and lust and care.

To him to love was natural as life:
He drew in passion with his daily breath;
Affection was his food, and hate and strife
To him the very atmosphere of death;
His soul was one of those to which the faith
In love and friendship is a part of being,
And—that withdrawn—there is for them no fleeing

From anguish and the death-stroke of despair:
Once hurt, they have but strength enough to die,
Since in life's desert there is nothing fair
For them, when love has lost its potency
And the first dream has vanished from the sky.
And so he loved as (men do say) of old
The first folk loved, within the age of gold.

There was no like respondence of delight
In fair Salvestra; for her weaker mood
Sufficed not for the all-subduing might
Of love that raged in his more ardent blood;
Her earthlier nature from that angels' food
Of perfect passion ever failed and shrank.
She knew not Love, though at her eyes he drank,

Though in her mouth his flowers were fresh and red,
His magic in each tangle of her hair
Was hidden; all was cold as are the dead,
And no one note of ecstasy was there,
To stir to splendour the unthrobbing air.
No glamours of the tender haze of love
Lay ever those clear orbs of hers above,

Such as are sweeter to a lover's gaze

Than brightest radiance of untroubled bliss—
No touch of tender sadness, such as lays
Soft lips to lips with such a rapturous kiss.
In her most glorious face, the soul did miss
The informing ardour of some subtle charm.
Whose absence chilled the Summer sweet and warm

That there bloomed ever: and the missing note
Left to the wish, in every harmony
Of loveliness that round her face did float,
A formless longing, as of some sweet sky.
In whose moon-flooded purple canopy
Of silver star-work set in amethyst.
The very star of evening should be miss'd.

They were alike unequal in estate.
His father was a merchant of renown.
That had held highest office in the state;
For whom a name of honour, handed down
Through many an ancestor, had slowly grown
And ripened to great increase of repute:
In him the tree had born its fairest fruit

Of worship. He had of his native town
Been three times prior: wealth and dignities
Had bound his temples with a various crown
Of splendid memories. His argosies
Had swept for treasure all the Indian seas.
Heaping his hands with gorgeous pearl and gold
And ingots cast in many an Orient mould.

So for Girolamo there was prepared
A goodly heritage, and his ripening age
Might to all heights of eminence have dared
To look for honour and all noble rage
For dignities have counted to assuage,
Being by birth set in that charmed ring.
Wherein the flowers of honour use to spring.

His foster-sister was that fairest one:
She was the daughter of a clothworker.
Unto whose wife his little weakling son.
Bom well-nigh in an equal hour with her,
Girolamo's own sire did, many a year.
Commit for fosterance; and so the twain
Together knew life's earliest joy and pain.

Surely some power had breathed strange spells on them.

To weave their fortunes in a mingled skein;
Some flower of Fate had blossomed on its stem
A double calyx, in some sweet domain
Of herbs and charms where (as old fables feign)
Fair wives do sit and weave with knitted flowers
The changeful fortunes of this life of ours;

With knitted wreaths, not woven all of rose
Or lavish jasmine in the gold of June
Or delicate sweetness of the flower that blows
In April, when the harsh winds breathe in tune
To Spring's fresh music and the ways are strewn
With violets. Rosemary is there and rue
And sad-eyed scabious with the petals blue.

There Cypress grows for garlands funeral
And there the dim and tearful lilies blow;
Sad hemlock for dead lovers' coronal
And nightshade, bitter at the heart for woe.
There not alone the lark and linnet throw
Spring's wealth of music on the enamoured air
And throstles sing that Summer is most fair;

But there full oft the widowed nightingale
Lengthens her holy sadness into song
And many a night-bird fills the air with wail:
Dead love sings there with cadence sad and long
And there the dread sweet tunes are dear and strong.
That in the hearts of weary folk are dumb;
Since sorrow is too fair to have outcome

In its most perfect strain from mortal throat
Or dare with its most holy notes and pure
The gross encounter of this world of rote,
Where men know not the sweets its pains procure.
So in this garden only doth endure
Divinity of sadness, 'mid the throng
Of joyful sounds a holy intersong.

Surely, the nymphs that wove the earthly fate
Of these two lovers,—whilst their white hands played
With amaranths and violets and the state
Of roses for the crown of youth and maid,—
Had heard these singing that the rose must fade,
Nesh violets wither from their fragrant bloom
Nor amaranths of love evade death's doom;

And sighing, laid a rose or two aside

And chosen herbs of sadness and of woe,
White wind-flowers and pale pansies, dreamy-eyed,
And evergreens of cypress, that do blow
When all green else has withered from the snow,—
Mindful that love is fed with Summer's breath.
But sorrow dies not, though the air be death.

The star of lovers, that upon the birth
Of these two lovelings shed its saddest rays.
Had bat thenceforward glimmered on the earth
A little span of nights and equal days.
When from his walking in the pleasant ways
Of life his father ceased and did commit
Unto his widow's care, in all things fit

For his son's heritage to govern him.
And she, a noble lady, fair and high.
Queenlike in goodly port and graceful limb.
But hard and stem withal, did her apply
Unto the matter well and faithfully.
Ordering his state and household passing well.
In all the things where need to her befell.

So for Girolamo the first years went
Peacefully by in pleasance and delight,
And all his years of youth he was content
To dwell with her his mother; nor despite
The heat of youthful blood, did aught invite
His peaceful thought to seek to be set free
From her control or larger liberty.

For such a perfect passion filled his heart,
So strong and therewithal so innocent,
That in his hope no thing could have a part,
Wherewith Salvestra's pretence was unblent;
And all his thought on her was so intent,
It seemed his youth should never pass away.
Whilst in her eyes love met him day by day.

He sought no fellowship with anyone.
Bearing no share in chase or revelry;
But in his love's companionship alone
He lived, disdaining all delights that she
Must leave unshared, and careful but to be
Beloved of her: for him, she being kind.
No other thing could touch his constant mind.

For him, the treasure of her love contained

And did annul with its most perfect light
All things for which he saw men sought and strained.
There was for him no other ear-delight
Than her sweet speech, no other charm of sight
Than her fair presence, and (she being gone)
No bliss save dreams of her from dusk to dawn.

His life to her was wholly consecrate;
She had no hope in which he did not share;
She was for either sorry or elate;
So twinned he was to her in joy and care.
It seemed as if some charm upon him were,
Whereby his soul its stature had forgone
And for pure love her weakness had put on.

How should a lover of such perfect fire
As this fair youngling, in the blush and heat
Of the first passion, find aught to desire
In her that lets herself be loved? So sweet
It was to love, he c6uld no more entreat
Than she would give him look for look and kiss
For longing kiss, and from the deep abyss

Of his unfailing passion could supply
Unconsciously the warmth that lacked in her,
Holding her coldness in such constancy
And ceaseless ardentness of love, the stir
Of the celestial flame that folded her,
Kissing her marble with ethereal fire,
Some semblance raised of its own pure desire.

And at her feet, in that unsullied time.
The golden harvest of his young life's Spring
He laid, outpouring all the lavish prime
Of his first hope, the bright ingathering
Of that clear time of youth, when every thing
Blossoms to beauty with the radiant hours
And all the thoughts are lovely unknown flowers.

He made his love for her one long sweet song
Of various cadence, filling every break
Of gradual rays with many a glittering throng
Of flower-new fancies, till, as some grey brake
From Spring's soft hands its robe of blooms doth take.
Her lesser life caught blossom at his smile
And was all glorified with love awhile.

So for a few sweet years their lives were blent

In mingled ways of love and innocence,
And no fear came to mar the sweet content
Of that untroubled season; but their sense
Slept in a linked enchantment, folded dense
And sweet as Summer-woods, that stand screen-wise
Betwixt the world and some dear Paradise.

(Ah lovely time of lave and purity!
April before the summer heats draw nigher!
What thing on earth is pleasant like to thee,
Whilst yet the veils lie folded round the fire
Of the insatiate conquering Desire,
When all things tremble with the dews of Spring
And love is mystery and wondering?

Ah! frail as sweet thy tender blossoms are,
Shortlived as primroses that blow in Spring
And die whilst yet the Summer shines afar
Nor May has set the swallows on the wing.
Thy strain is as the birds' descant that sing
In haunted woods a dreamy song and clear
And cease, if any stay his steps to hear.)

For years, none knew the bondage of delight
That bound these lovers (nor themselves as yet
Perchance had learnt to name their ties aright;)
But unobserved of any eye they met
And took their ease of kiss and amorette;
Till, at the last, chance broke the happy spdl
Of secrecy; and on this wise it fell.

The palace, where for many years bygone
His ancestors had dwelt, a little space
Without the city's ramparts stood withdrawn,
Fronting the silver river with the grace
Of its tall turrets, wreathed on every face
With flowers and shrubs, through which the white house shone
Like some dream-stead the sunset lies upon.

Hard by the house a little wood there was,
Tow'rd which the garden sloped its slow descent
Adown long sunny banks of smoothen grass,
With chalices of Summer thick besprent;
And through the sward a silver brooklet went
And made sweet music to the amorous breeze.
Until it wound among the shadowing trees.

Full of bird-song and scent of forest-flowers

The coppice was, and very sweet and cool
In the hot noontide were its trellised bowers.
Set by the glass of some dream-haunted pool.
Whereon the sleepy sweetness of the lull
Of silence brooded; and its every glen
Was set with purple of the cyclamen

Or starred with white of amaryllis blooms,
Pale flower-dreams of the virginal green sward.
That made faint sweetness in the emerald glooms:
And through the stillness ever rose and soared
The song of some up-mounting lark, that poured
The gold of his delight for rose-hung June
Into the channel of a perfect tune.

Here did these lovers often use to walk.
Calling the flowers to witness of their love,
Mocking, in sport, with sweet and murmurous talk,
The tender cooing of the amorous dove.
That filled the arches of the boughs above
And echoed through the cloisters,—sat anon
Upon some lilied bank and there did con,

In rapturous silence, every lovely look,
Each blush of eloquent cheek and glow of eyes,
Reading sweet stories in that lovers' book
Of joining faces, with soft wind of sighs
To fan their joyance,—as a breeze that dies.
Bending two neighbour roses till they meet,—
And now all sunned with laughters low and sweet

It chanced, one Summer, as the lovers went
For joyance in the pleasant woodland ways,—
Rejoicing in the tender thymy scent
And in the sweet attemperance of the blaze
Of noon that reigned within the forest maze,—
The Countess walked, for ease of the fierce heat,
In that fair garden, where the lawns were sweet

With lavish fall of rose-leaves; and anon
The cool sweet promise of the wood did woo
Her feet to enter where the sunlight shone
Athwart thick leafage and the sky showed blue
Through rifted boughs; and walking thus, she knew
The sound of voices mingled in converse
Murmurous and sweet, as birds that did rehearse

Some new sweet descant for the ear of night:

And listening closelier, as the voices drew
The nearer, she was ware that Love's delight
Was theme of that soft speaking and she knew
The silver speech of kisses, that ensue
The vows of love, as music follows on
With strain on strain, in some sweet antiphon;

And curious to know what folk these were,
That walked in woods for love and solacement,
Under the shadow of the boughs drew near
Beside the shaded path, where, all intent
Each upon each, hand-linked these lovers went:
So low they spoke, she could not catch their words
Aright, for chatter of the clamorous birds

And gurgle of the stream betwixt the trees.
But in the middle way the sun had found
A place of branches rifted by the breeze
And stealing through the opening to the ground,
Had thrown a pool of golden light around;
And as the twain passed where the sunlight shone,
She recognised Salvestra and her son.

Then much despite gat hold upon her soul
And sorely she was troubled in her mind;
For shame it seemed to her and bitter dole
That thus a low-born maiden had entwined
Her son with arts; and sore she sought to find
Some means whereby he should be won to break
The chains he wore for sweet Salvestra's sake.

Crouched in the shadow of the thick-set leaves.
She waited, while the twain passed on their way
Out of the wood; and where the forest-eaves
Bent o'er the highway, there she saw them lay
Lips unto lips, as 'twere the last that day:
And then they parted, she toward the town
Wending, with hasting feet and girded gown.

But he a little stood, with longing eyes
Following her form along the highway's white,
Until,—when all the power in Love that lies
Availed not to retain her in his sight,—
Sighing as one that lapses from delight,
He pushed the gate that opened from the street
And wandered up the garden with slow feet

And wandering thus, he came to where the fount

Smote the blue air with one thin silver spire
And in like gracious fashion did dismount
Into the jewelled pool, that lay afire
With golden carp,—and rising again higher,
Did seem to image some fair perfect love,
That, lowlier stooping, soars the more above.

And there, beside the tinkle of the stream.
Himself he laid upon the rose-strewn grass
And in the sweet ensuing of his dream
Of bliss, saw not his mother that did pass
Swiftly by him, with mien and look, alas!
That of a truth forebode despite and ill
To that fair love which all his thoughts did fill.

(Ah, Love! Ah, fair god Love! it wearieth me
To think haw many work to do thee ill,—
How many in this grey sad world there be
That strive alway thy gracious power to kill
And hinder those that do thy gentle will!
Forsooth, it is great wonder that away
From earth thou hast not fled this many a day.

For of a truths fair God, my soul is sad
For these two lovers and the coming blight
That those who hate thy gentle spells and glad
Have conjured up to slay their hearts' delight;
And sore it irks me that the goodly light
Of such a sweet Spring-day should change and fade,
For men's despite, to death's unfriendly shade.

And yet take heart, God of the soul's delight!
No hate shall slay thy tender empery:
The day is not more sure of the sun's sight
Nor Spring of flowers, than that there aye shall he
Maidens and youths to offer prayers to thee—
Ay, sure as death,—and singers, too, to sing
In every age of Love's fair triumphing.

So, in all lovers' names and in the name
Of all true men that set their hearts to song,
I lay a life-long curse on those that frame
Sad wiles and false to poison Lave with wrong
And wear out passion with the anguish long
Of partings—ay, grey life I invoke for them
And death unsanctified by requiem

Of choiring linnets. Never flower of Spring

Shall blossom in their lives, nor fruit of peace
Ripen their summer long to harvesting;
But with the years their sadness shall increase
And shadow them: and when dull life shall cease,
Their heads shall lie unmemoried in the gloom,
Nor lovers wander by their flowerless tomb.)

But that fair haughty lady, being come
Into the house, began to cast about
Within herself to bring to pass the doom
Of parting for these lovers: without doubt
It seemed to her, that if she opened out
Her mind to him, he could not choose but bow
Unto her will, as always until now.

But first, intent upon a milder way,
She sought Girolamo and so began
To work toward her wish with words that lay
Like foam upon the waves and overran
Her purpose, saying that well-nigh a man
He now was grown and how the need was great
That he should presently to man's estate

Advance himself in things of daily use
And knowledge of the ways and works of men,
To end that he might fit himself to choose
Some station in the world, coming to ken
All things wrought out with sword and speech and pen
And all the stir of folk, that day by day
Beat up the wave of life to foam and spray.

And meet it seemed (to him she did pursue)
That for the better ripening of his youth
In all things liberal and knowledge due,
He should leave idling in that sunny South,—
That treacherous mother with the red bane-mouth,—
And for awhile in lands of colder air
Temper his thought and learn new senses there.

But he took little heed of her discourse.
Hearing her speech but as a devious dream,
That through the channels of a sleep doth course,
With trains of doubtful words, that do but seem
And leave no memory by the morning's beam;
And all the while he answered not or made
Some mutter of reply, that nothing weighed.

Till, for her useless wiles, the pent-up spite

Began to break the chains of prudentness.
And with harsh words unto the hapless wight
She did pour forth her heart's full bitterness
Against Salvestra and her rage no less
Against himself, upbraiding him full sore
For those fond foolish fetters that he wore:

And ended by commandment laid on him
That he should do her bidding in this wise
And for awhile,—until the thought grew dim
Of that his folly,—under foreign skies
Avoid the witchcraft of Salvestra's eyes;
So haply, being come to man's estate.
He should have wit to choose a worthier mate:

And adding many a false and feignèd tale,
She did oppress his sad and aching ears,
Until at last with lies she did prevail
Upon her son to yield his will to hers
And lose his lady's sight for two long years,
Wherein she hoped Salvestra should be wed,
Or else the love of her in him be dead.

Therewith Girolamo, enforced by guile.
Took leave of that fair Florence and the sight
Of his Salvestra,—and full many a mile
Journeying by land and sea, unto that bright
And goodly city came, that Paris hight.
Wherein all loveliest ladies use to dwell
And many a fair lord of whom men tell.

For, of a truth, in that fair country France
Has ever been the home of love and song:
There knights have done fair deeds with sword and lance;
And if by hazard any suffer wrong,
I' faith therein he shall not suffer long,
Nor any lady lack to be redrest.
Whilst any lord of France have spear in rest

And verily, if they be brave and fair,—
The knights and damozels that dwell therein,—
The land is beautiful beyond compare
And worthy of its children: therewithin
The earth is thick with lilies and the din
Of nightingales and every sweet-voiced bird
All night among its rose-gardens is heard.

And of that goodly land, the pearl of flowers.

The queen-rose of the garland Paris is,
Paris white-walled, that from its fragrant bowers
Rises tall-steepled, full of pleasaunces
And gardens sweet with jasmine and with lys
And palaces that glitter in the air.
Less fair alone than ladies dwelling there:

Paris, whose life is like a dream-delight
Of splendid memories, where the very walls,
(Mowing with old-world splendours, charm the sight
With tales of hero-life; and trumpet-calls
Re-echo from the golden-fretted halls.
Telling how women loved and men were strong.
And poets set their lives in golden song.

(Ah, land of roses! France, my love of lands!
How art thou fallen from thy high estate!
Bleeding, thou writhest in the Vandals' hands
And the crowned spoiler sitteth in thy gate.
My heart is sore for thee: I weep and wait;
Shall not God help thee and deliver thee
From whom the world has taken liberty?

Thou France, the fairest and the holiest,
The knightly people, hating every wrongs
Hast thou so long redeemed the world opprest,
Sacring the Right with sword and sword-swift song,
Hast thou so many a year for us been strong
To slay the doubt, to unveil the hopeful years,
And now, alas! sittest alone in tears?

Alone and bleeding; for the Wrong prevails,
The dragon-crested Wrongs that, like a snake,
Growing, shall strangle in its loathsome scales
All loveliness of life, all hopes that break
The grinding chains of toil, all songs that wake
Under the flower-blue skies, all knightly use
And level all to its abhorred abuse.

For this is he that in the name of Right
Has strangled many a nation; this is he
That holds all noble faith, all honour lights
That let the lust of his rapacity;
He that, exulting from a bloody sea.
Calls God his helper; he that, void of shame,
Robs, lies and murders in the Holy Name.

Alas, that men are blind or will not see!

Our Saviour France, the lever of mankind,
Lies bound and bleedings straining piteously
Against the brutal tyrant: on the wind
Her cries for help assail us; but we, blind
With some prophetic blindness, turn aside,
Sayings, She sinned; her doom let her abide!

And yet take hearty O land of many tears!
We are not powerless that love thee well:
Our songs float up to Heaven and God hears
Our psalms of vengeance. Fair and terrible,
The hour shall come to break the evil spell:
Live I for we love thee. Shall not love be strong?
Arise and conquer, fortified with song!

Our love thy banner! We are manifold:
Though men contemn us, we are strong in faith,
We that are taintless with the greed of gold,
We for whom Love is mightier than Death;
We hail thee with a hope! As with one breathy
We bid thee conquer—spite the scorn of men—
And slay the twy-necked Vulture in his den!)')

Two dragging years, two full-told weary years
In that fair town Girolamo did dwell
Unwillingly,—for all his mind with fears
Was racked, and on his thought the cruel spell
Of some vague misery lay and made a hell
Of every thing and every pleasant spot,
Where the fair face of her he loved was not.

Nor was there any damozel so fair
Of all the lovely ladies that he saw
Walk beautiful about the gardens there
Or ride a-hawking in green field and shaw.
That could anew subdue him to Love's law:
He counted all their lovely looks for nought,
For his love's face was ever in his thought.

And so, when those two weary years were past,
Wherein he had been exiled from delight.
And he was free to turn his feet at last
To Florence, well I wot his heart was light.
To think he should regain Salvestra's sight;
And not a thought of sorrow held his mind,
For all the pleasant things he left behind.

But, with a heart inflamed with long desire

And love that on itself so long had fed.
That it had taken for its food of fire
All other thoughts, across the sea he sped
And came to Florence, wearying to tread
The earth that bore Salvestra and to press
Once more within his arms her loveliness.

Alas! he thought not what a hapless thing
Is absence and how easily far love
Is apt to fall off from remembering.
Knowing there was no creature fair enough
Nor any chance that could prevail above
The fortress of his heart, how should he fear
Less constancy in her he held so dear?

So, when he knew, as very soon he knew,
(Ah me, ill hap hath no relenting wing!)
That she, by whom alone the sky was blue
And the day sweet to him,—dishonouring
Her plighted faith to him,—was wed with ring,
The fulness of his misery smote him not
At first. As one that in the heart is shot

So suddenly that at the first he seems
Untouched by wound, yet presently he falls
Stone-dead,—or like a man that walks in dreams
And sees each thing that unto him befalls
As others' fortune,—through the palace-halls
He went, all dazed, among old memories,
As one that looks and knows not what he sees.

And at his heart some vague disease did gnaw,
Sapping the springs of life, so that he cared
For nought nor took delight in aught he saw
Or heard; but like a soul in doom he fared
Aimlessly here and there, and no man dared
To stay his feet or strive to comfort him;
For all his gentle visage pale and grim

Was grown; and if one spoke to him, he gazed
A moment in his face with witless eyes.
But answered not and left him all amazed.
Even when his mother pressed him,—weary-wise
He broke from her, filling the air with sighs:
And for the indulgence of his lonely mood.
He did betake himself into the wood.

And there, at last, the sweet familiar dells

And woodways, where he wont to walk of old
With his Salvestra, and the rewrought spells
Of birds' descant and flowers and summer-gold.
Wherewith his happy memories were enscrolled,
(That now, alas! were poison), broke his trance
And made him ware of all his heavy chance.

And when at length the full and fatal sense
Of all his misery possessed his brain.
The anguish of wanhope was so intense,
That his weak body failed him for the pain:
Well-nigh it wrought to break the enfeebled chain
Of life; and in a fever, many a day,
Nigh unto death unconsciously he lay.

But yet the strength of his supreme desire
Once more to look upon his lady's face,
Mightier than death, prevailed against the fire
Of that fell sickness: with a halting pace,
Sad life came back to its accustomed place
And from his bed he rose, a weary man.
Wasted with fever, pale and weak and wan;

And for the staying of his longing pain,
Bethought him first where he might chance to meet
Salvestra's eyes and hear her voice again:
For he could not believe, the memories sweet
Of the old time and all their ancient heat
Of love could fail to stir her heart and bring
Her soul back to him with remembering:

Nor could he think, still less, that she had proved
False to her faith of her unfettered will;
But rather deemed that she to it was moved
By force or by some sad disloyal skill
Of slander, that so many loves doth kill,—
And doubted not, in spite of all the let
Of years and duties, but she loved him yet

For all the wealth of love bestowed on her
And garnered up within his heart so long
Seemed surety to him that there yet must stir
Some love in her, unknown belike, yet strong;
And as within the bird's throat sleeps the song.
Dumb for captivity, that yet the view
Of all his native woods would wake anew.

So, at his sight, he could not choose but deem.

The old frank faith would wake in her afresh.
And like the tangles of some doubtful dream,
She would shake off from her the weary mesh
Of falseness and her eyes on his afresh
Rain love and truth, her lips once more rejoice
Him with the constant sweetness of her voice,

Renewing the dissevered bonds of love:
And then the days of doubt should pass away
And be but as some mist that hangs above
The certain summer of an August day,
A little while, and tempers the sun-ray,—
And all the ancient bliss return to him,
A brighter noon because the dawn was dim.

Wherefore he set himself to haunt the ways
Where she was wont to pass,—the market-place,
The square before the church on holidays,
The paths tree-shadowed and the flower-set space
Beside the river,—watching for her face
Morning and noon and night, as one in pain
Looks for the face of Death; but long in vain.

At length, at the church door he met with her,
Leant on her husband's arm and listening,
Well-pleased, to what he whispered. Lovelier
She seemed than she of his remembering
Unto Girolamo; and a double sting
Ran through his heart, to look on her so fair
And know those fatal charms another's were.

By him, held dumb by hope and fear, she past
And by some hap, chancing to lift her eyes,
Straight on his face her starry glance she cast
And looked at him a space; but in no wise
Her lover's form she seemed to recognise,
(Perchance for he was still with fever wan)
But saw him as a stranger and passed on.

Full long, I ween, he deemed his death at hand.
Being (it seemed) of his last hope deprived;
But once again the expiring spark was fanned
Into a flame, (so strong a hope is hived
In lovers' breasts) and there once more revived
The wish of life in him, that he might prove
To end the doubtful fortune of his love.

For it might be (his hope 'gan whisper him)

That she had looked on him and known him not,
Seeing he was so changed in face and limb
By that fell fever, or some spell had got
Empire on her, whereby she had forgot
The memory of their wooing and the face
Of him her lover, for a little space.

And if (as well he deemed that it might be)
Some fatal charm were laid upon her sight,
He trusted to dispel that sorcery
By prayers and offerings and the happy might
Of counterspells; and thus, the sad despite
Of fortune foiled, she should possess again
Her memory and take pity on his pain.

Wherefore by day and night long prayers he prayed
To many a saint, and to that Lady bright.
That rules the skies, rich offerings he made.
To gain her grace, sparing not day or night
To crave her intercession to relight
The old love in Salvestra, nor did cease
To wear her chapel's marble with his knees.

Nor did he trust alone in stress of prayer
To break the sorcery of that opiate spell;
But every occult influence did he dare,
Invoking the divided powers of Hell
To heal her blindness whom he loved so well.
Culling night-herbs and on a scroll blood-writ
Burning strange cipherings beyond man's wit

And then, at last, when every prayer was vain
And no spell seemed to stand his hope in stead.
Seeing she passed him often and again
And gave no sign of cognizance, but sped
Upon her way with an averted head,
And not a word or look of hers exprest
Renewal of his image in her breast,

He would not even then lay hope aside.
But comforted himself, despite his pain,
With the firm thought that there must needs abide
Some memory of him within her brain.
Which though his sight had foiled to wake again,
(Being, as he was, so changed and strange to her)
The cadence of his speech should surely stir.

And so about within himself he cast

How he should win to have her privately
To speak with him, proposing in this last
Attempt to set his life upon the die;
But often as Salvestra passed him by
In streets or on the church's steps of stone,
He could not win to speak with her alone.

Wherefore, made bold by his supreme despair.
He did resolve to seek her, spite of all,
Even in her husband's house, and being there,
To make one last endeavour to recall
Her love to him, whatever might befall;
And if, alack! his prayers should find no grace.
He might at least die looking on her face.

He knew her husband was a tent-maker
And dwelt, with many others of his trade.
In a long street, that folk for many a year
Called "Street of Tentmakers." At back there strayed
The river; and between, long gardens made
A pleasaunce for the burghers, very fair
With tree-shade and the river running there.

Thither one afternoon he did betake
Himself, what time the sultry Summer day
Grew faint and in the flower-beds and the brake
The fierceness of the sunlight died away.
Beneath a starry myrtle-bush he lay
And watched the glitter of the noon subside,
Across the running ripples of the tide.

And there, unseen, he waited, purposing,—
When night was fallen on the scented air
And once the nightingales were waked to sing,—
To make his secret way (if means there were
And night were favouring and debonair)
Into Salvestra's chamber and contrive
At least to speak with her once more alive.

Full wearily the unwilling day wore on:
It seemed to him the light would never die:
Across the west like blood the sunset shone;
And to his sense, as sadly he did lie,
The wafts of air seemed laden heavily
With incense for the dying and the surge
Of ripples sounded like a funeral dirge.

At length the lagging daylight made an end

Of gradual death; and to the grateful night
He heard the sweet sound of the bells ascend
From many a convent-steeple in his sight;
The dusky town put forth pale buds of light;
He heard the throb of lute-strings, and afar
The silver chirp of some soft-swept guitar.

Then from his bed among the flowers he rose.
And with the careless step of one who dares
A lawless act and heedeth not who knows.
Being so sick at heart that nought he cares
For aught that can befall him, up the stairs
Of stone he went and pushed against the door.
That swung ajar, yielding his hand before.

And entering, through the humble rooms he went.
Noting the traces of Salvestra's hand.
That everywhere some grace of neatness lent
To the poor dwelling. Here, a little stand,—
Wherein tall lilies, twined about a wand.
Hallowed the air with perfume,—there, the gold
And silver of the jasmine-blooms, enscrolled

About the little casement,—told their tale
Of her sweet ministry; and with each trace
Of her, fresh anguish did his heart assail.
To think another's home possessed her grace,
Another's hearth was lighted by her face:
And haply had he chanced her then to meet.
He might have fallen lifeless at her feet

But all alone about the house he trod.
And no one stayed or asked him what he did;
For so it chanced, Salvestra was abroad.
With Paolo her husband. Unforbid,
He wandered sadly here and there, amid
The tokens of her presence, without aim,
Until into her bed-chamber he came.

There freshlier still the signs of her abode
Did crowd on him; the ribbon that she wore
For festivals, the shining glass that showed
Her eyes her beauty,—all the pretty store
Of women's toys: and eke the table bore
A silver rose he gave her on its stem,
When love was in the summer-time for them.

The pretty bauble's sight brimmed up his eyes,

At the sad thought that such a toy should keep
Its pristine brightness, when his Paradise
And all the roses of his hope so deep
In death did sleep the unremembering sleep;
And oft with many kisses did he press
That senseless relic of past happiness.

At last he heard a footstep on the stair
And ran to hide himself behind a heap
Of tent-cloths standing in a comer there.
Thinking concealed there himself to keep,
Until, perchance, when Paolo should sleep.
He might come forth and gently her awake:
And haply she on him would pity take

Nor rouse her sleeping husband, but at worst
Give ear to his sad pleading for the sake
Of all the gentle memories of erst:
Mayhap, the cruel ice in her should break
And some soft pity at the least awake
In her, so she should speak some kindly word,
Which he might die more gladly having heard.

The chamber-door swung open and she came,
One hand about her husband's neck entwined;
Whilst, in the other hand, the taper's flame
Leant to the lazy flutter of the wind:
And as its flickering gleam upon her shined.
It seemed the amorous shade did strive for place
With the dim light, upon her lovely face.

The weary wight, tired with the sultry day
And the long labour, on the couch flung down
His stalwart limbs, and soon asleep he lay:
But she, unfastening her tresses' crown.
Let down their sable flood, that all did drown
Her form, until she gathered them again
And set her to comb out each silken skein.

Lingering awhile before her glass she stood,
Joying to look upon her lovely face,
And with a musing sweet content reviewed
The perfect harmony of every grace:
Then, with unhasting hands, each envious lace
She did unloose, that bound her body fair.
And stood all naked in her floating hair.

(Ah! not for me her loveliness to sing

And the rich sweetness of each pearly limb!
My song would droop its slow and faltering wing,
Did I enforce its weakness to that hymn
Of silver splendours or my pen to limn
The sweet snows of her breast and the delight
Of her clear body's symphony of white.

I would I could command his lyre of gold,
That sang that Marie loved of Chastelard,
Or his full harp, that of fair Nyssia told,
Guarding her jealous beauty like a star,
Or else his silver lute, whose ladies are
Florise and Cypris and that Goddess bright
That leads the silver lapses of the night.)

Alas! my heart is sore for his despite
That saw his love, that never should be his.
Then first unveil her beauties to his sight!
It was as if before some soul, that is
In flames of hell, a dream of heaven's bliss
Were conjured up to mock his anguished sense
And make his thought of horror more intense.

He would have called to her,—but could nor speak
Nor move; it seemed some strange and fettering swoon
Compelled his sense, so sick he was and weak
With waste desire. Till she put off her shoon
And covering the lamp, let in the moon
That filled the chamber with its argent tide;
Then laid her by her sleeping husband's side.

Now was the hour at hand when he should prove
The last device of his resolved despair:
And yet awhile he could not win to move.
But gazed full long upon her sleeping there,
Pillowed within a fragrant cloud of hair.
With parted lips and heaving breasts, that shone
Like lilies on a lake by moonlight wan.

At last he did shake off the numbing spell
That held his sense in bonds of stirlessness;
And from his place he crept with feet that fell
As noiselessly as fairies' feet that press
The dewdrop grass. The room was shadowless;
Her husband slept the heavy sleep of toil;
And the void lamp had wasted all its oil.

Upon his knees beside the bed he sank,

As one that kneels before a virgin shrine,
And with long looks of yearning sadness drank
Her lovely sight All bathed in white moonshine,
Stirless she lay; and on her lidded eyne
Such peace abode, one might have deemed it death,
Save for the fluttering witness of her breath.

At length, with tremulous touch and wavering,
His hand he laid upon her ivory breast.
That for a moment stayed its fluttering
And throbbed uneasfly, as if opprest:
But yet therefore ceased not Salvestra's rest;
So feather-light his tender touch did lie,
She did but flutter out a gentle sigh.

Then, bending o'er the cover of the bed.
He set his lips upon her sleep-sealed eyes
And eke upon her mouth's twin flowers of red,
As softly as a fallen flower, that lies
And floats upon a river, lily-wise.
Still did she sleep; and he, grown bolder still.
Of clinging kisses took his thirsty All.

Ah, when was lover true yet satisfied
With lovers' food of kisses warm and sweet?
He would have kissed and kissed, until there died
The life in him; but, as his lips did meet
And clung to hers more close, the sudden heat
Quickened the throbbing pulses of her heart
And forced the ivory gates of sleep apart

Her heavy lids drew up and loosed the light
Captive within their envious prison-sleep;
And as his kneeling figure met her sight,
The drowsy sweetness, that her eyes did steep.
Into a pretty fearfulness did leap;
And for her sheer affright she would have cried.
But in her throat the words sank down and died.

For in his face, bent down towards her own.
The lamp of such a perfect love was lit.
And in his sad dear eyes the peace alone
Of such a loveful gentleness was writ.
She could not seek for any fear in it,
But lay and looked on him, with still surprise
Rounding the sleepy sweetness of her eyes.

Then, "Sleepest thou, my love of loves?" he said:

And at his voice, the thoughts, that in her breast
Had for long absence and the years lain dead,
Upon her in a crowd of memories prest
Like birds returning to their last year's nest,
The words and deeds of the sweet time of yore
Rose up and lived before her thought once more.

And with the memory, such a fretful tide
Of struggling fancies did oppress her brain,
That for relief aloud she would have cried
And help; but as to speak she strove in vain,
He spoke once more and prayed her to refrain,
For 'twas Girolamo, whom she had loved,
In the old days, alas! so far removed.

Then with soft words to her he did recall
The linked delight of those unsullied days.
When each to each was lovers' all in all
And wrought with other in Love's pleasant praise.
Heart joined to heart; and in all tender ways
Love could contrive to work upon her grace.
He did entreat her fairly to retrace

The vanished paths of faith, to turn aside
From the deceitful ways in which her feet
Had lately wandered,—since false lips had lied
Surely to her of him,—and once more greet.
With those long looks of love that were so sweet.
His thirsty eyes, that had of her fair sight
Bereavèd been so many a day and night.

And with full many a piteous device
He strove to turn her heart again to him
And conjure back the lovelight in her eyes,
Recounting how, when absence was so grim
And sad to him, her face had ne'er grown dim
Within his memory, but, clear and fair,
The thought of her was with him everywhere.

And how all fairest ladies of the land.
Where damozels are loveliest, had failed
To move the heart he left within her hand.
And how no pleasant sight or sport prevailed
To win his thought to gladness, that bewailed,
'Mid proudest feast and music's silveriest swell.
His banishment from her he loved so well.

Nor did he fail to paint his great despair

And all the springs of life dried up and waste.
And how for him thenceforth no thing was fair
Enough, no joy of living could he taste.
That might retain his weary soul, in haste
To break die chains of that abhorrent earth,
Her love alone made fair and worship-worth.

For of a surety (and he showed his face.
Wan-white with sickness, and his sunken eyes,)
The life should linger in its weary place
Small time after the new day's sun should rise,
Unless her hand reknit the severed ties.
That to his spirit only peace could give.
And her lips' honey lent him strength to live.

So he poured prayers into her listening ears;
And all the while her hand in his he held.
Bathing its ivory with the bitter tears.
Which from his breast so thick and fiercely welled.
That now and then to pause he was compelled;
And as he ceased, upon her hand he poured
Kisses more eloquent than any word.

And for awhile it seemed to him, the strength
Of his despair prevailed upon her soul;
For her lids quivered and adown the length
Of her soft cheek a silver tear did roll
And a half sigh out of her bosom stole;
And as upon her hand his lips he prest,
He heard the heart throb loudly in her breast

Alas! his hope was all in vain. Full soon
She drew her hand out from between his own
And trembling, as one waking from a swoon,
Conjured him, for God's sake, to get him gone
And leave her quiet—else she were undone:
For of a truth the day was near to break,
And momently her husband might awake.

"For in those ancient foolish days," she said,
"We were but girl and boy and in child-guise
Did use to kiss and toy with each and played
At love and courtship, for no harm might rise
Of such child's sport: but now 'tis otherwise;
For years have passed away since that befell
And I am married, as thou knowest well.

"And ill it should become me to the love

Of any other man to give consent
Than this my husband; wherefore, if there move
Within thee any fear of God or saint,
I do entreat thee now to be content
With that which thou hast dared and done to night.
And get thee gone before the day grow white.

"For but consider what a cruel wrong
Would fall on me through thine unmeasured heat.
And how the harm to me would be life-long.
If day should come and find thee at my feet
Now is my life happy and calm and sweet;
For Paolo my husband loves me well,
And in content and peace with him I dwell.

"But if by evil chance he should awake
And see thee kneeling thus by my bedside,
He would leave loving me for thy rash sake
And all my happy days with strife be tried;
So that no more in peace I could abide
With him,—even if no other harm ensue:
Wherefore, I prithee, this I ask thee, do.

"Or if the thought of ill to hap to me
Avail not to avert thy wanton will.
Bethink thee that no hope can ever be
That any act of mine shall aye fulfil
Thy mad desire or that there lingers still
A spark of love for thee within my heart
Thanks thou shalt have, if but thou wilt depart"

(Ah me, what misery can equal his,
Who loves and hears his dearest love confess.
With that sweet voice that conjures back old bliss.
The sad impeach of cold forgetfulness!
I wot there is no pang of hell nor stress
Of endless death, that can prevail above
The wistfulness of unrequited love.)

So knelt Girolamo, and listening
To those cold words from that belovèd mouth,
That did close up for him the gates of Spring
And all the golden memories of youth.
Knew all his hope in vain and felt the growth
Of that cold bringer of the eternal rest
Stir in the silent chambers of his breast.

But even while he felt the chills of death

Creep through his heart, he could not choose but take,
(So strong is Love and such charm lingereth
About the loved one's presence!) whilst she spake.
Some sad delight Even though his heart should break
At her harsh words, the sweetness of her voice
Could not but make his faithful soul rejoice.

But when she ceased the music of her speech.
The spell dissolved from him, and he awoke
Unto his full despair nor did beseech
Her any more nor strove again to evoke
The phantom of dead love. The heavy stroke
Was merciful and did benumb his brain,
So that he thought no more to strive in vain.

Nor did he find it in him to upbraid
Her cruelty; but with a weary air
And a sad voice, that might not be gainsaid,
He did entreat of her one little prayer
Of his to grant and lighten his despair; —
That she would let him in the couch, beside
Her body warm, a little while abide.

For all the heat had left him, with the chill
Of the night-air;—and swore to her to lie
Silent by her nor touch her, but quite still
And mute to bide the while;—and presently,
(He did avouch) before the day drew nigh.
As soon as he regained a little heat,
He would arise and go with noiseless feet

Then she,—some little moved by his despair
And haply thinking thus the quicklier
To be relieved of him,—unto his prayer
Consented and did let him lie by her.
Enjoining him to lie and never stir.
And when as she should bid him go, that he
Should rise and get him gone immediately.

But he, his weary body being laid
Within the bed, began to ponder o'er
Within himself the things that she had said;
And in his thought revolving all the sore
Sad end of every pleasant thing of yore
And all the grief that in his heart did lie.
He presently resolved himself to die.

So, with one last fond look at her sweet face,

That lay beside him with averted eyes,
And one last prayer to Mary full of grace
And one last Ave intermixed with sighs,
He folded up his hands to sleep, childwise.
And by his dearly-loved Salvestra's side.
He rendered up his gentle soul and died.

So lay Girolamo the while the hours
Slid onward through the cloisters of the dusk:
And now the day began to put forth flowers.
Pale buds of morning opening from the husk
Of the small hours; and all the lights, that busk
The cheerless heavens in the earliest dawn,
Grew grey and chill across each upland lawn.

And as the earliest dawn-streak in the East
Began to glimmer through the casement's glass,
Salvestra started from her fitful rest;
And gradually, what had come to pass
That night recalling to her mind, "Alas!
The dusk is burning to the break of day,"
She said, "and yet Girolamo doth stay!"

Then did she chide him for his broken word
And did conjure him rise without delay
And get him gone. Yet not a whit he stirred,
But dumb and motionless as death he lay
And gave no heed to aught that she could say;
Till she, supposing him with sleep opprest.
Stretched out her hand and touched him on the breast.

But lo! her passing hand aroused him not;
And to her touch, as cold as any ice
His bosom smote. A deadly terror got
A sudden hold upon her. Twice or thrice
She called him by his name. Then did she rise,
And bending o'er him, felt no stir of breath
Nor throb of pulse and knew that it was death.

Then such a deathly fear laid hands on her
And such an icy coldness of dismay,
That for awhile she could nor speak nor stir;
But by the dead all tremblingly she lay;
Whilst through the clouds the grey and early day
Crept from the casement to the dead man's place
And threw a ghastly light upon his face.

Then gradually the thoughts began to take

Some form in her; and she was sore afraid
Lest Paolo her husband should awake
And find a lifeless man beside her laid;
For much she feared lest he should her upbraid.
Seeing the grisly sight would surely move
The man to deem her faithless to his love.

And in her thought awhile considering
How she should best avert the blame she feared.
At last she did resolve to tell the thing
Unto her husband as a story heard
In idle talk or else a chance occurred
To other unknown folk, and so to know
Whether the thing should anger him or no.

Then, waking him, as if by accident.
She did relate to him how, in a dream.
So strange and sad a thing to her was sent.
That still before her mind's eye it did seem
To be presented, and (as she did deem)
Till she had told him all, it would not cease
To weary her or leave her any peace.

Then, in ambiguous words (concealing nought
Save name and place) the fatal circumstance
Of all the ills to that sad loveling wrought
By love, she told him,—how a youth did chance
To love a maid, and being sent to France,
After two years returned and found her wed,—
And how, in his despair, beside her bed

By night he knelt; and finding every prayer
For love's renewal vain, did beg to be
Allowed to warm himself from the cold air
A little by her side. To which prayer she,
Moved by his grief to pity, did agree;
And how, when he had lain awhile and said
No word, she had awoke and found him dead.

And as she made an end of saying this.
She prayed him he would tell her, of his mind.
Whether the wife therein had done amiss,
And what the husband, who awoke to find
A stark dead man beside his wife reclined,
Should do. Whereto he answered, that the man
Must hold her blameless, since, as woman can.

She had resisted all her lover's suit;

But that, before the folk began to go
About the ways, whilst yet the streets were mute,
He should, to avert the evils that might grow
From slanderous tongues—if any came to know
The thing—take up the dead, and through the town
Bearing him, in his doorway lay him down.

Whereat Salvestra, being lightened much
At heart to hear him speak his mind so fair
And righteous, took his hand and made him touch
Girolamo his bosom lying there
Stark dead and cold; whereby he was aware
She had made known to him, in other's name,
Her own mischance. Yet not a word of blame

To her he said, but rather comforted
Her timorous soul and bade her have no care.
Then, rising straight, he lifted up the dead
And on his shoulders through the streets he bare
Girolamo's sad body to the stair
Before his mother's palace in the town
And there all reverently he laid it down.

Now, when the day was wakened with the sun
And men began about the streets to go,
One of the Countess' servants saw her son
Lie as asleep within the portico,
And touching him, to know if it were so,
Found that the life from its sad seat had fled
And told his mistress that her son was dead.

Then she, for pride repressing her despair,
Shed not a tear; but, with a pale set face,
Commanded instantly that they should bear
The body to the chief church of the place
And set it by the Virgin's altar space,
That there all due observances might be
Filled, as behoved his rank and ancestry.

So, with the majesty of funeral rites,
They bore Girolamo unto the fane
And there, amid a blaze of votive lights,
They set his senseless body down again;
And with full many a prayer and many a strain
Of ceremonial song, they did commend
His soul to God: nor did they make an end

Of mourning him; but, as the manner is.

When any noble dies, they did bewail
His piteous death and loss of earthly bliss
In earliest youth: and soon the sorry tale
Of all his heavy fortune did not fail
To stir among the people gathered there
And move their hearts to pity his despair.

Now, when the news was come to Paolo,
Girolamo his body had been found.
Most earnestly he did desire to know
What talk might be among the folk around.
And to what cause—seeing there was no wound
Upon the man nor of disease a sign—
His strange and sudden death they did assign.

And to this end, Salvestia he enjoined
To mingle with the women at the door,
Within the church, and hear what tale was coined
Among the folk, and thus herself assure
That he had been unnoticed—when he bore
The body home—of any citizen:
And he would do the like among the men.

The thing he bade was pleasing unto her,
For (such a doubtful thing is woman's mind)
The pity that his love had failed to stir
Within her bosom, while the Fates were kind.
Possessed her now; and she, that could not find
A gentle word to gladden him alive,
Felt for the dead the ancient love revive.

So with a trembling step she bent her way
Toward the church; and when afar she saw
The dead man's face across the dense array.
Love took revenge of his contemnèd law,
And such invincible desire did draw
Her feet unto the place where he was laid.
She rested not until her way she made

Athwart the crowd and stood beside the bier;
Then, with a haggard eye considering
The sad sweet face furrowed with many a tear
And worn and wasted sore with sorrowing.
The thought of his despair prevailed to bring
To pass what all his life had failed to impart
And Love gat hold upon her stubborn heart.

Awhile she stood, with haggard straining eyes

And hands that seemed to stretch toward the dead.
As if to conjure back from Paradise
The gentle soul from the sad body fled;
Silent she stood, and not a tear she shed:
But her face bent toward him more and more
And her drooped knees sank slowly to the floor.

At last her swelling bosom found a vent
For all its weight of anguish and despair;
And with a cry that all the silence rent
And stirred the calling echoes far and near,
She fell upon his bosom, lying there,
And kissed the cold lips and the death-sealed eyes
And called upon him madly to arise.

For Death could surely have no power on him,
Seeing she loved him with so fierce a heat;
Her kiss should surely from the very rim
Of the black night recall his wandering feet
But none the less the white face cold and sweet
Lay passionless, the pale lips answered not
And all her blandishments availed no jot.

Then, gradually, seeing that in vain
Her tardy kindness came, nor all love's stress
Availed her to reknit life's severed skein,
She did abate for very weariness
Her idle strife and lay all motionless:
But still with one long kiss her hot lips clave
To his cold mouth that none in answer gave.

And thus awhile she lay, her haggard face
Pressed unto his that died for love of her.
Whilst on the floor her locks did interlace
With the full golden clusters of his hair.
Long time she lay on him and did not stir;
And on the air there hung a ghastly spell
Of silence, measured by the tolling bell.

At length, the pitying folk that stood around
And wept for dolour of that piteous sight,
Thinking Salvestra fallen of a swound,
Would have uplifted from the marble white
Her senseless form; but when they brought to light
Her lovely face, they found the sweet soul fled
And knew these lovers for waste love lay dead.

So Death took pity on ill-fortuned love

And at the last did grant these lovers twain
That boon all other earthly bliss above,
At rest beside each other to be lain
And never stir from their embrace again.
Ah Love! thou art full sweet; but never yet
Did any man of thee such guerdon get.

And there they buried them beneath the trees.
Beside the running river, breast to breast.
These two sad lovers. Ladies, if it please
Your gentle hearts to hear of folk opprest
Of love, I pray you use it softliest,
This little song of mine, and say with me,
God save all gentle souls that lovers be!

Ah me! shall Love for ever suffer wrong?
Shall none avail to stay the steps of Fate?
Since Summer and its roses and the song
Of choiring birds are powerless to abate
The conquering curse, the uncompassionate;
But all themselves must seek that frozen shore
Where Spring and all its flowers have gone before.

Alas! meseems there is none other thing
Assured to us that work and watch and weep,
Save only memory and sorrowing
And the soft lapse into the eternal sleep!
The harvest that we sow, what hands shall reap,
What eyes shall see the glories that we dream,
What ears shall throb unto the songs we deem,

We know not; nor the end of love is sure,
(Alack, how much less sure than anything!)
Whether the little love-light shall endure
In the clear eyes of her we loved in Springy
Or if the faint flowers of remembering
Shall blow, we know not: only this we know —
Afar Death comes with silent steps and slow.

Men lay their lives before the feet of Love,
Strewing his way with many-coloured flowers,
And poets use to set his praise above
All other rulers of the days and hours:
From age to age untold, recurrent showers
Of psalm and song attest his empery
And crown him God above all Gods that be.

And with an equal breathy on that dark Lord,

That rules the going out from life and lights
The hate and fear of men have been outpoured,
In words that borrowed blackness from the night;
Nor have the singers spared with songs to smite
His silent head, styling him bitterest foe
Of that fair God that myrtle-crowned doth go.

And yet, what Love could not prevail to do,
Companied round with every goodly thought
And every happy chance that men ensue,
When all his charms of flowers and birdsongs wrought
And all his sorceries availèd nought
To give t/use lovers peace and twinned delight—
That Death wrought out of his unaided might.

And thou, O best-belovèd of the sad,
Deaths the angel of the end of tears!
Let those heap blame on thee, whose lives are glad,
For wham thy dwelling is the dusk of fears.
I praise thee, that have loved thee many years:
Though men revile thee, thou art dear to me:
Sad is my song; I bring it all to thee.

For me, I love thee not for lives beyond
The compassed darkness of the accomplished Fate;
I look not, I with dazzled eyes and fond,
To find new worlds behind thine iron gate;
I love thee for thyself compassionate;
I seek thee not for heavens and new life,
Only for thine embrace that shuts out strife.

I look not, I, for the awakenings
After long sleepy in brighter worlds to come;
I look but for the end of wearying,
For pain to cease and sorrow to be dumb;
To lay me down, with stricken sense and numb,
Hiding my weary face within thy breast,
Rest in thy bosom, and around thee rest.

But you, my Masters, in whose mighty track
I have ensued with slow and faltering feet,
I will crave pardon of you, if I lack,
In this my song, to follow on the beat
Of your firm footsteps—if my errant heat
Have, in the sad enchantment of my days,
Put off the strong assurance of your lays.

And first, glad Mastery standing with one foot

On earth and one foot in the Faery land—
Whose song, with virgin Una taking root,
Branches, a forest-tree majestic, spanned
From earth through heaven unto the elfin strand—
Thou that didst count the seasons and the hours
With the fair forest calendar of flowers,

That knew'st no sadness, building up thy song
With love and life and deeds of high emprise,
That rod'st with cheerful heart the world along,
Counting to crown fair life with Paradise—
I pray thee, Master fair and glad and wise,
To pardon me, if none of these I seek;
For I am sad, alas! and very weak.

And thou, O star-browed singers-folded round
With the vague awe of the Invisible,
As with a cloak—whose radiant front is crowned
With triple coronals ineffable,
Attesting the assay of heaven and hell—
Thou, whose aspèct indeed is very sad,
Yet therewithin the hope of heaven had

Burns like a glory and a shining fire —
O pilgrim of the high celestial town,
Forgive my weakling thought, if it aspire
Not to the palm-branch and the starry crown,
Only the soft rest and the lying down
To dreamless sleep and cease of sorrowing;
For I am weak and ask a little thing.

A little things a narrow sorry hope!
Indeed, a little thing to look upon,
If one be glad and in the Future's scope
Long vistas of fair places to be won
And valorous deeds for doing follow on,—
A weary hope, i' faith, if one be strong
And run the race in gladness and with song.

But, if the life be grief in any one
And his despair shrink from the face of light.
Fearing to see the splendour of the sun—
If day for sadness wither in his sight
And his tears fill the watches of the night,
If love be madness and the hope of men
Seem to his soul a mockery,—ah, then

He cares not to renew the weariness

Of unspent life within the years unknown;
He shall not seek the never-ending stress
Of the sad days for him immortal grown,
A palace where his soul shall walk alone;
His heart inspires but to the end of pain,
The sleep where morning never comes again.

And thus I hail thee, Lord of all my lays!
Master and Healer, coming with soft wing!
I lift my feeble voice unto thy praise,
For thou to me art hope in every thing.
Others have glory and remembering,
Fair hope of future life and crown of faith,
Love and delight; but I, I have but death.

Wherefore I praise thee, seeing thou alone,
Of all things underneath the heavens born,
Art all assured. For is it not unknown
Whether the glad sun on another morn
Shall glitter or the Spring come to adorn
Once more the woods and fields with winter pellet
This but we know; thou Death shall never fail.

And unto thee I bring this weakling song,
(For I am thine, and all my little skill)
Wherein, alone among the busy throng,
I have enforced me sadly to fulfil
My meed of thanks to thee,—and loudlier still
My growing voice shall praise thee, Death, than now.
Lord of the Future, certain only thou!

John Payne – A Concise Bibliography

The Masque of Shadows & Other Poems (1870)
Intaglios; Sonnets (1871)
Songs of Life and Death (1872)
Lautrec: A Poem (1878)
The Poems of François Villon (1878)
New Poems (1880)
The Book of the Thousand Nights and One Night (1882–4) A translation in nine volumes
Tales from the Arabic (1884)
The Novels of Matteo Bandello, Bishop of Agen (1890) A translation in six volumes
The Decameron by Giovanni Boccaccio (1886) A translation in three volumes
Alaeddin and the Enchanted Lamp; Zein Ul Asnam and The King of the Jinn: (1889) editor and translator
The Persian Letters of Montesquieu (1897) Translator
The Quatrains of Omar Kheyyam of Nisahpour (1898)

Poems of Master François Villon of Paris (1900)
The Poems of Hafiz (1901) A translation in three volumes
Oriental Tales: The Book of the Thousand Nights and One Night (1901) A translation in fifteen volumes
The Descent of the Dove & Other Poems (1902)
Poetical Works (1902) Two volumes
Stories of Boccaccio (1903)
Vigil and Vision: New Sonnets (1903)
Hamid the Luckless & Other Tales in Verse (1904)
Songs of Consolation: New Poems (1904)
Sir Winfrith & Other Poems (1905)
Selections from the Poetry of John Payne (1906) selected by Tracy and Lucy Robinson
Flowers of France: Romantic Period (1906)
Flowers of France, The Renaissance Period (1907)
The Quatrains of Ibn et Tefrid (1908, second edition 1921)
Flowers of France: The Latter Days (1913)
Flowers of France: The Classic Period (1914)
The Way of the Winepress (1920)
Nature and Her Lover (1922)
The Autobiography of John Payne of Villon Society Fame, Poet and Scholar (1926)

www.ingramcontent.com/pod-product-compliance
Lightning Source LLC
Chambersburg PA
CBHW060101050426
42448CB00011B/2576